THE NOTEBOOK OF DOOM

DAY OF THE NIGHT CRAWLERS

by Troy Cummings

BRANCHES™
SCHOLASTIC INC.

Read more books in

THE NOTEBOOK OF DOOM series!

#1

#2

#3

#4

TABLE OF CONTENTS

To Professor Klaus: Good luck to you in your various undertakings.

Thanks again, Katie Carella and Liz Herzog, for your patience, hard work, and impeccable ability to improve everything I throw your way.

Cummings, Troy.
Day of the night crawlers / by Troy Cummings.
p. cm. — (The Notebook of Doom ; 2)
Summary: Alexander and his new friend, Rip, are worried that the worms the rain has brought out are really the megaworms that Notebook of Doom describes but they soon discover that the night crawlers are trying to warn them about the monster tunnel fish that are threatening Stermont Elementary.
1. Monsters—Juvenile fiction. 2. Worms—Juvenile fiction. 3. Fishes—Juvenile fiction. 4. Elementary schools—Juvenile fiction. 5. Horror tales. [1. Monsters—Fiction. 2. Worms—Fiction. 3. Fishes—Fiction. 4. Elementary schools—Fiction. 5. Schools—Fiction. 6. Horror stories.]
I. Title.
PZ7.C91494Day 2013
813.6—dc23
2012050301

ISBN - 13: 978-93-5103-450-6

Book design by Liz Herzog
First Scholastic printing, September 2013
This reprint edition: March 2026
Printed in India at Shivam Offset Press, New Delhi

CHAPTER 1

A NICE, WORM BREAKFAST

Look out, Al. . . . Here comes a monster!”

“Where?!” cried Alexander. A week ago he would have thought his dad was joking. But now, after moving to Stermont, he couldn’t be sure. This town was packed with monsters.

“RARRR!” Alexander’s dad said, handing him a plate. “A *breakfast* monster!”

Alexander sighed.

"Sorry there's no mouth on this breakfast monster, but I didn't have any bacon," said Alexander's dad. "Now chow down! I have to fetch the newspaper before it floats away!"

Alexander glanced out the window. It was pouring.

CLACK. As soon as Alexander heard the front door close, he pulled a beat-up notebook out of his backpack.

The old notebook had a creepy-looking skull and the initials *S.S.M.P.* on the cover. Alexander had been studying this notebook ever since he'd found it. The book was full of drawings and facts about monsters.

Alexander wasn't sure who had started the notebook, but last week he'd written his own entry after defeating an army of balloon goons. Alexander could still hardly believe that the dancing, wiggling, arm-waving balloons were actually monsters!

Alexander snapped the book shut as his dad came back in, sopping wet.

His dad tossed a soggy newspaper onto the table.

Drops of water splashed onto Alexander's plate, along with something long, pink, and wiggly.

"Yuck — a worm!" Alexander yelled.

"It's just a night crawler," said Alexander's dad.

Alexander put his fork down. "I think I'm full now," he said.

Alexander stuffed the notebook into his backpack. "I should get to school," he said. "I'm walking with Rip." At first, Alexander had thought Rip was a bully. But now they were friends.

"Okay, Al. Stay dry!" His dad mussed his hair.

Alexander opened the front door. The storm clouds made everything seem gray — except for the ground. The ground was sort of pinkish.

As Alexander stepped out onto the front porch, he could see why.

Everywhere he looked — his yard, his driveway, the sidewalk — little pink night crawlers were wriggling. Thousands of them.

"Ugh," said Alexander. The only thing squirming more than the worms was his stomach. He opened his umbrella and headed out.

CHAPTER 2 RAIN, RAIN, DON'T GO AWAY

Alexander tiptoed down the rainy sidewalk.

He made his way to a playground where his friend Rip was sloshing around.

"Hey, Salamander!" Rip shouted.

Salamander was Alexander's nickname, whether he liked it or not. He sort of liked it.

"Wanna see something gross?" Rip asked. He raised a boot over one of the squirming worms.

"Rip, no!" said Alexander. "Don't!"

Rip lowered his foot a little. "They're just worms! What's the big deal?"

Alexander sighed. "Rip, when we fought those balloon goons, we helped

everyone in Stermont — even these tiny worms. If we go around squishing 'em, we're no better than the monsters we were trying to stop!"

Rip made a gagging sound. "Fine," he said. "But it's weird to be surrounded by worms. I feel like a meatball wading in spaghetti!"

"You're right, Rip." Alexander's eyes grew wide. "This *is* weird. Super weird!"

He pulled the notebook out of his backpack.

"The notebook!" Rip said. "Hey — what does S.S.M.P. stand for, anyhow?"

"I don't know yet," said Alexander. "But look! There's something in here about worms!"

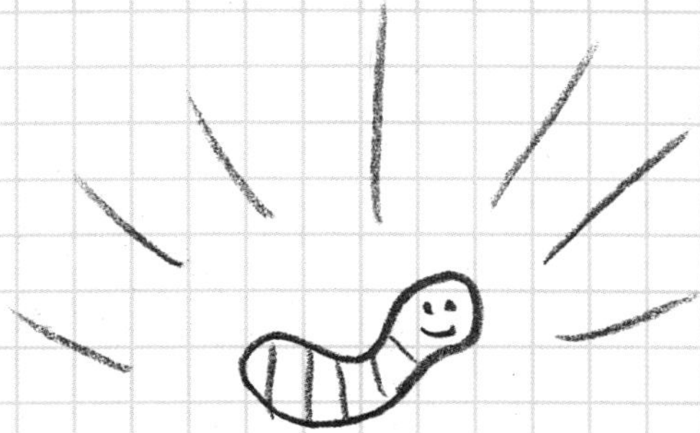

MEGAWORM

A small blue worm that seems harmless. At first.

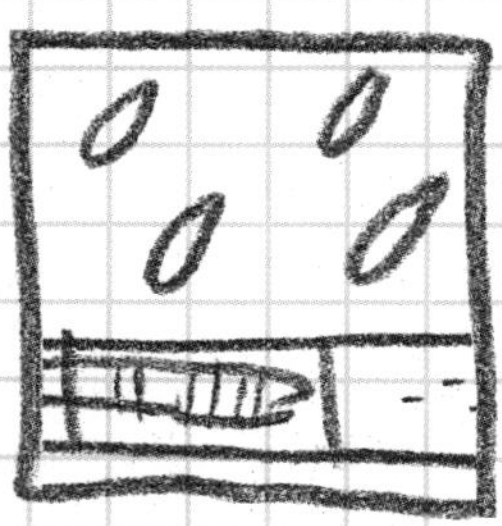

HABITAT Megaworms can be found on wet ground and sidewalks.

BEHAVIOR Megaworms always travel alone.

DIET Unknown. Possibly eats kids.

POP! Megaworms smell like caramel corn.

WARNING! A megaworm starts out tiny, but grows bigger than a school bus when sunlight hits it. Keep megaworms out of the sun!

BEFORE AFTER

WEAKNESS Any kind of loud screeching sound makes them shrivel up.

"This can only mean one thing," said Alexander. "These night crawlers must be megaworms!"

"Yeah . . ." said Rip. "Wait — no! That notebook says megaworms travel alone." He pointed the umbrella toward a nearby heap of worms. "There must be *millions* of these guys. There's no way they're megaworms!"

"But what if you're wrong?" asked Alexander. "What if all of these worms grow huge and start eating kids?!"

Rip shrugged. "The monster notebook also says megaworms are blue — but these worms are pinkish gray!"

Alexander held up a finger. "Then let's do a test!" he said. "A screech should shrivel them up." He squatted down near a worm, took a deep breath, and —

The worm wiggled a little.

Rip tugged at Alexander's elbow. "C'mon, Salamander. Let's get to school."

"Well, okay . . ." said Alexander. "Maybe Mr. Hoarsely can tell us about these monsters. Remember what he said at my birthday party?"

"Yeah," said Rip. "He said that those balloon goons were only the beginning."

"I just wish we knew what he meant. . . ." said Alexander.

CHAPTER 3
DIAL *H* FOR HOARSELY

SWISH! The Emergency Room doors opened as Alexander and Rip entered the old hospital building, which was now their school.

A tall man with tall hair was leaning on the front desk. He was putting on a pair of sneakers.

"Mr. Hoarsely!" Alexander called. "Worm monsters are attacking Stermont!"

"Maybe," Rip added.

"SHHH!!" Mr. Hoarsely said, looking around.

"I *know* there are monsters here, but the worms —"

"Right — the worms!" said Alexander. He gave Rip an I-told-you-so look.

"I'm sorry," Mr. Hoarsely said. "I need to make an announcement." He picked up a microphone.

"Testing . . ." he said. The speaker on the wall was silent. He flipped the switch to INSIDE. "Good morning, students." His voice sounded shaky. "Since it's such a rainy and, uh, wormy day, we'll be having gym indoors."

“Okay, Mr. Hoarsely,” said Alexander, “what about these megaworms? If we don’t stop them before the sun comes out, they’ll —”

“Look,” Mr. Hoarsely said, putting a whistle around his neck, “I’ll see you in gym class. I really need to —”

“Eep!” Mr. Hoarsely jumped. He picked up the phone. “Stermont Elementary, no longer Stermont General Hospital. May I help you?”

Alexander whispered to Rip, “Gym class? Wait — isn’t Mr. Hoarsely the school secretary?”

“Yeah,” Rip said, “but he’s also the gym teacher, the nurse, and a bus driver. The school is saving money by —”

"WHAT?! NO!" Mr. Hoarsely screamed into the phone. "I'm not going to fight *you*!"

Alexander glanced at Rip. Rip shrugged.

"NO!" Mr. Hoarsely lowered his voice. "Um, could you hold?" He pressed the HOLD button.

"Boys," Mr. Hoarsely said, staring dead ahead, "get to class." He hunched over the phone and returned to his call.

"But if sunlight hits those worms, Stermont is toast!" said Alexander. Rip shook his head and dragged Alexander toward the elevator.

The sky outside was still cloudy. For now.

CHAPTER 4

RETURN TO SENDER

Alexander and Rip walked into their underground classroom, which used to be the hospital morgue. Now instead of being a place for storing dead bodies, it was a place for storing bored students.

"If it isn't the Tardy Boys!" said a short man wearing three kinds of plaid.

"Morning, Mr. Plunkett," Alexander said to his teacher.

He found a seat in the back, next to a girl in a hoodie. She was the only kid who had been nice to him on his first day of school.

"Um, hi," Alexander said.

She was busy reading a book and didn't seem to hear him.

Alexander took out his monster notebook and flipped to the megaworm pages. *How can I stop them?* he thought.

The hoodie girl turned her head a little.

Is she peeking? worried Alexander. He quickly turned to a different page to hide the megaworm pages.

KOALA-WALLA-KANGA-WOMBA-DINGO

HABITAT These monsters are found beneath the bathroom sink. Or below the couch cushions. Any place that's down under.

FLOOSH! Toilets flush counterclockwise when K.W.K.W.D.s are nearby.

DIET Boomerang-shaped food: bananas, croissants, squash, etc.

BEHAVIOR Koala-walla-kanga-womba-dingoes love to cuddle.

WARNING! It's a trap! As soon as you touch a koala-walla-kanga-womba-dingo, a joey will pop out of her pouch and nip your nose. Anyone bitten by a joey instantly becomes Australian.

Alexander closed the notebook. *Too bad we're not under attack by cuddly koala-kanga-whasits,* he thought. *I'd take those over megaworms any day.*

"Students," said Mr. Plunkett, "today's lesson will be entirely about worms." The hoodie girl was opening her science book.

Alexander jotted a note on a scrap of paper, folded it, and handed it to the hoodie girl.

"Pass this to Rip," he whispered.

She nodded and sent the note along. After a few passes back and forth, their conversation filled the page.

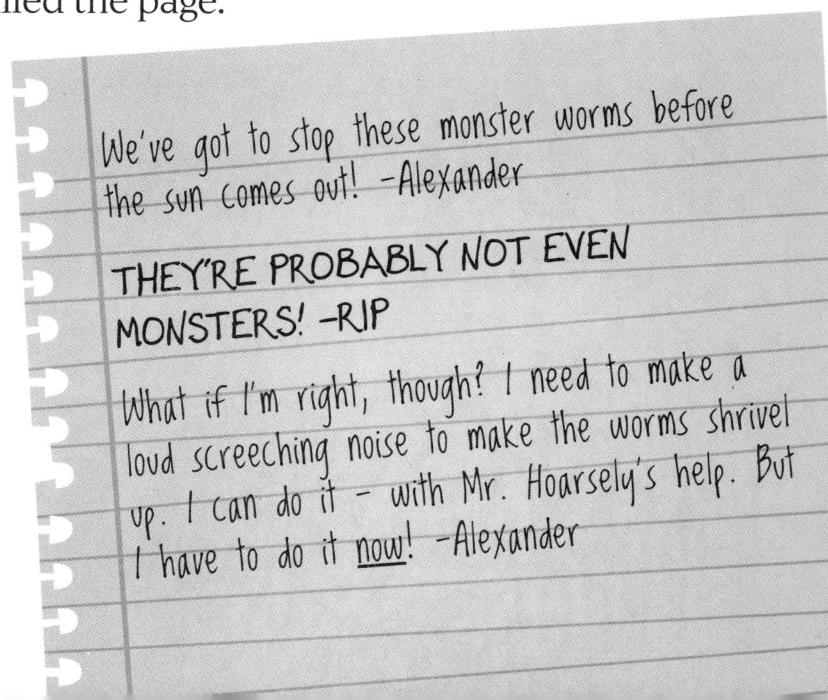

SO DO IT ALREADY! —RIP

But how do I get out of class? -Alexander

Just ask for a bathroom pass! —Nikki

STAY OUT OF THIS, NIKKI! Salamander, just ask for a bathroom pass. —RIP

Alexander sat upright. "*Nikki?*" he said aloud.

The girl next to him tugged on her hoodie strings.

"Excuse me, Alexander," said Mr. Plunkett. Everyone turned to look. "Do you have something to say?"

"Um, I, yes —" Alexander glanced at Nikki and Rip. "I've got to go to the bathroom. It's an emergency!"

Mr. Plunkett scratched his mustache. "Okay. Come get a hall pass. You've got five minutes!"

Alexander took the hall pass and ran. He knew just what he had to do. . . .

CHAPTER 5

SCREEEECH!

Like a secret agent in sneakers, Alexander crept through the empty cafeteria. Some lunch ladies — and a lunch man — were busy cooking something green with purple chunks.

Or is it purple with green chunks? thought Alexander.

A small blackboard hung on the wall.

Alexander took down the blackboard.

Okay, he thought. *I just need to bring this to Mr. Hoarsely and —*

DING! The elevator doors slid open.

Alexander dove behind a fake fern, almost dropping the blackboard.

"— and here we have the last part of our tour: the cafeteria," said Principal Vanderpants.

Alexander peeked over the fake fern. Ms. Vanderpants came out of the elevator, followed by a masked woman in padded clothing.

"Terrific," said the masked woman. Or maybe she had said "Jurassic." Her voice was muffled by the mask.

"I'm pleased you could fill in on such short notice," said Ms. Vanderpants. "It's unlike Mr. Hoarsely to just disappear."

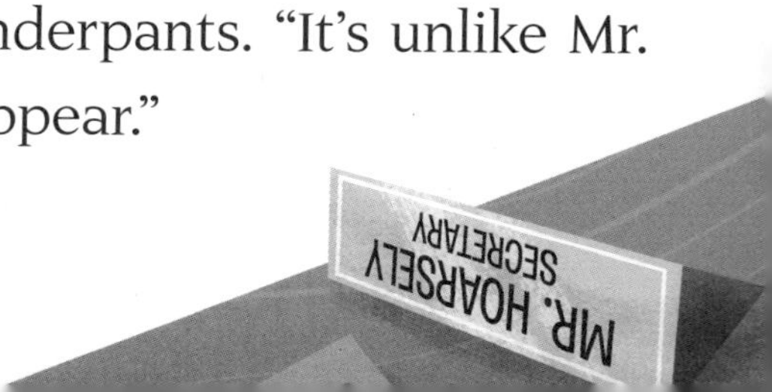

Disappear? thought Alexander.

The two women walked into the cafeteria. Alexander clutched the blackboard and slipped into the elevator just before the doors closed. He pushed **1** for the first-floor lobby.

DING! Alexander burst out of the elevator.

He looked out the lobby window: The ground was carpeted with night crawlers. The sky was still overcast, but the clouds were thinning out.

He sprinted to the front desk. "Mr. Hoarsely! I need your —"

Alexander stopped short. The desk was a mess. Papers were scattered about. The phone was off the hook. And Mr. Hoarsely was not there.

Alexander picked up the receiver. "Hello?"

Silence.

Alexander hung up the phone.

Mr. Hoarsely has *disappeared,* he thought. *And it looks like he left in a hurry!*

The room brightened. A sunbeam broke through the clouds, shining on the worms below.

"No!" Alexander lunged across the desk and grabbed the microphone. "Take this!" he yelled, raking his fingernails across the blackboard.

SCREEEEEECH!

A terrible sound thundered through the building.

Oops, thought Alexander. The microphone was still set to INSIDE.

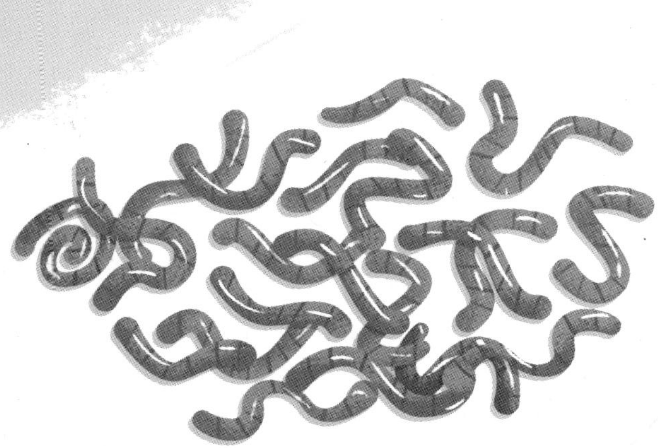

DING!

The elevator doors slid open. "Alexander!" Ms. Vanderpants rushed out. "We do not *play* on the intercom!"

Alexander quickly flipped the switch to OUTSIDE and scratched the blackboard again.

SCREEEEECH!

He looked out the window. The night crawlers were now bathed in sunlight. But they just kept wiggling. None of them grew as big as a school bus, and none of them ate anyone.

I was wrong, thought Alexander. *They're just plain old worms.*

He relaxed a little. "Everyone's going to be fine," he said.

A firm hand squeezed his shoulder.

"I don't think *everyone's* going to be fine," said Ms. Vanderpants. "My office. Now."

CHAPTER

6 TABLE FOR THREE

By the time Alexander made it to lunch, the cafeteria was out of green stuff. They were just serving purple chunks.

He took a seat next to Rip.

"That was a super-long bathroom break," Rip said, winking.

"Yeah, Ms. Vanderpants was pretty mad," said Alexander. He sniffed a purple chunk. "You know, I've never been in trouble like that before."

"You get used to it after the first six or seven times." Rip chugged his milk. "So . . . About those worms . . ."

"Okay, okay — you were right," Alexander grumbled. "They were just regular night crawlers."

"Poor Salamander . . ." Rip smiled. "It must be hard being friends with a smart guy like me!"

Alexander swallowed a mouthful of chunks. "I was wrong about the worms, but there *are* more monsters in Stermont. Mr. Hoarsely said —"

"Monsters? What are you two talking about?" Nikki set her tray on the table and sat down.

"None of your business," Rip growled. "Now bug off!"

Nikki turned to Alexander. "So, how did everything go with the worms?"

"Uh, fine." Alexander frowned. "I guess."

They all stared at the table.

"Lunchtime is over," Rip said, glaring at Nikki. He turned to Alexander. "Let's go, Salamander. I'm sure Hoarsely will fill us in during gym."

"Oh!" said Alexander "I almost forgot — Mr. Hoarsely is missing! I overheard Ms. Vanderpants telling some weird lady about it."

"Really?" asked Nikki.

"He probably got spooked by his own shadow," said Rip. "I bet he's hiding in a locker, waiting for gym class to start."

"I sure hope you're right," said Alexander. "I've got a lot of questions for him."

CHAPTER 7 SWORD OF A BIG DEAL

"Wait up, Rip!" said Alexander as he pulled on his gym shirt.

Alexander walked into the gym. Actually, it wasn't a gym — it was a hospital laundry room.

Students had lined up near a row of washing machines. Everyone wore matching gym clothes, except for Nikki. She joined Alexander and Rip at the end of the line.

"You wear your hoodie to gym?" Alexander asked.

"Yes." Nikki jammed her hands into the hoodie's pockets. "I have a . . . condition."

"What do you mean?" asked Alexander.

CLANG! CLONG!

The students stopped talking. "What was that?" someone whispered.

Alexander pointed to a square hole in the ceiling. "It's coming from the laundry chute!"

BUMPA-BUMPA-BOOM!

"Is someone up there?" asked Nikki.

"Duh, Nikki!" Rip sneered. "I bet that chute is Hoarsely's hidey-hole!"

The clanging sound grew louder until — **WHOOSH!** — a white blur tumbled through the chute. The blur caught a water pipe and flipped backward through the air,

landing perfectly on its toes.

Whoa! Alexander took a step back. It was the masked woman he'd seen earlier.

The class started clapping.

"She's an acrobat!" said Nikki.

"Acrobat, nothing," said Rip. "She's a *ninja*!"

The woman took a bow.

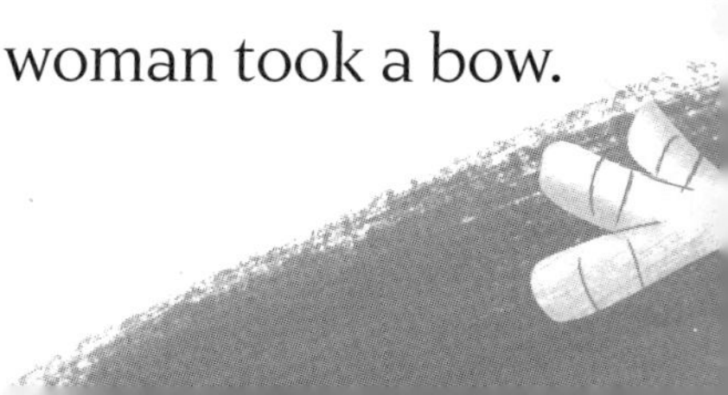

"Good afternoon, students. I am Coach Gill." Her voice sounded wet and bubbly, like she was gargling mouthwash. "I'll be filling in while your teacher is . . . on vacation."

Alexander raised his hand. "But Mr. Hoarsely isn't —"

Coach Gill leaped across the room and landed in a crouch, inches from Alexander.

"Yes?" She read Alexander's shirt. "Mr. Bopp? Were you going to correct me on the whereabouts of" — she took a raspy breath — "Mr. Hoarsely?"

Alexander stared into Coach Gill's face mask, but all he could see was darkness. He also caught a whiff of her breath. *Pee-yew! Someone had tuna for lunch!*

"Um, no," he said, leaning back. "Never mind."

Coach Gill stared at Alexander a moment longer.

"Today," she said, "you will learn the sport of warriors — fencing!"

She wheeled out a laundry cart full of swords. "Everyone, take a practice foil," she said. "Once you've sharpened your skills, you may one day use a real blade. Like mine."

Alexander tapped Rip's shoulder. "Doesn't her sword look weird?"

Rip didn't answer; he was busy swishing his foil around. "This is so cool! I can't believe we're sword-fighting!" he yelled.

Coach Gill flicked her sword — **CLACK!** — knocking Rip's foil to the floor.

"It's *fencing*, not sword-fighting," she said.

"Everyone, watch." She jumped up onto a laundry-sorting table. "Stand like this. And hold your foils like this."

The students waggled their foils.

"Terrible!" Coach Gill screamed, looking directly at Alexander. "You've got 24 hours to shape up. There'll be a quiz tomorrow. CLASS DISMISSED!"

CHAPTER 8 IN THE LOOP

After school, the sky was still partly cloudy and the ground was still partly wormy.

"There are fewer night crawlers than before," said Alexander.

"You're right," said Nikki. "I wonder where they — *oof!*"

She had stumbled over a mound of dirt.

"Watch out for molehills," she said, pointing to a second dirt pile.

Rip walked behind Alexander and Nikki, swinging his practice foil. "It's so awesome we get to take our swords home!"

Alexander rubbed his chin. "Don't you think Coach Gill is kind of . . . strange?"

"No way!" said Rip, slicing at the air. "She's great!"

"But what about her mask?" asked Alexander. "She never takes it off — even outside of class."

"Coach Gill is a *professional*!" Rip lowered his foil. "You wouldn't understand, unless you were into sword-fighting."

"You mean *fencing*," said Nikki.

"Eat worms, weirdo!" Rip yelled.

"Guys! Stop!" Alexander said. "Look!" He pointed to the sidewalk. Dozens of night crawlers had twisted themselves into a loopy squiggle.

"Whoa," said Rip. "It's some kind of secret code."

"That's no code," said Alexander. "It's fancy lettering! The worms are writing something." He squinted. "Can you guys read cursive?"

"Nope," Rip said. "They don't teach cursive at Stermont Elementary."

"I can read it," Nikki said.

"What?" Rip snapped. "If *I* can't read it, then neither can you!"

"Sure I can," Nikki said. "I learned cursive *years* ago."

Rip cocked his head. "Years ago? Baloney! That's —"

"Great!" said Alexander, putting a hand on Rip's shoulder. "So, Nikki, what are the worms trying to tell us?"

Nikki peered at Alexander from under her hood. **"Beware! The fish are coming!"**

CHAPTER 9 FISHING FOR ANSWERS

Despite the night crawlers' weird warning, Alexander, Rip, and Nikki all had to get home for dinner.

Alexander dropped his backpack as he came in the door.

"Son?" said his dad. "Have you been battling fearsome enemies?"

"Dad — I can explain! Those balloon goons were —"

"Balloons?" His dad chuckled. "I was thinking pirates — or musketeers!" He pointed to Alexander's backpack.

Alexander exhaled. "Oh, that!" He yanked out his practice foil. "That's just homework."

He bounded up the stairs. "Call me when dinner's ready!"

Alexander sat down at his desk and made a list of questions and clues.

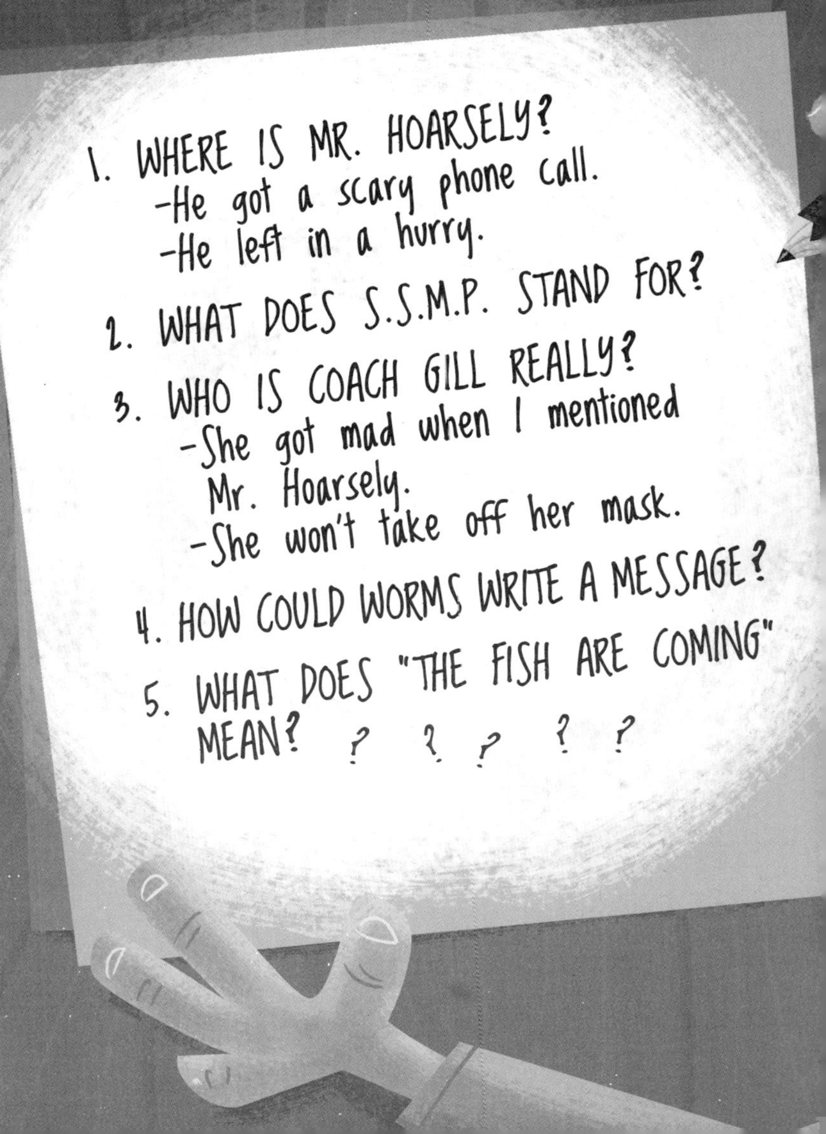

1. WHERE IS MR. HOARSELY?
   - He got a scary phone call.
   - He left in a hurry.
2. WHAT DOES S.S.M.P. STAND FOR?
3. WHO IS COACH GILL REALLY?
   - She got mad when I mentioned Mr. Hoarsely.
   - She won't take off her mask.
4. HOW COULD WORMS WRITE A MESSAGE?
5. WHAT DOES "THE FISH ARE COMING" MEAN? ? ? ? ? ?

The fish . . . thought Alexander. *Wasn't there something about fish in the notebook?* He turned past the mostly ripped-out first page and began thumbing through the book.

He stopped at a page filled with fish. *This is it!* he thought.

TUNNEL FISH

A creature that can "swim" underground. It drools A LOT, which loosens the dirt, making it easy to dig.

SIDE EFFECT Tunnel-fish slobber makes night crawlers super smart, allowing them to read and write.

TEE-HEE! Tunnel fish have ticklish tongues.

HABITAT Dirt, soil, mud. Not cement.

DIET Anything smaller than itself. When tunnel fish are near, worms flee to the sidewalks for safety. Tunnel fish will sleep for 99 years after a big meal.

WARNING! Don't get tunnel-fish drool on you – it's super-gross!

Tunnel fish! thought Alexander. *Tomorrow, I'll —*

"Dinnertime!" called Alexander's dad.

Alexander ran downstairs. His mind was racing so much he could hardly eat his pizza.

"All right — all done!" Alexander said, wiping his mouth.

"Hold on," said Alexander's dad. "I've got a surprise for you. Catch!" He tossed a round red object across the table.

Alexander caught it. "A yo-yo?"

"Yep!" his dad said. "Yo-yos are prizes for my patients — to reward them for flossing. Neat, huh?"

"Yeah," said Alexander. "Well, good night!"

He headed upstairs, tossing the yo-yo into his backpack on the way.

Unfortunately, Alexander was so excited about the tunnel fish that he forgot to floss.

CHAPTER 10 DIG IT!

"Ha! Take that!" Rip yelled, practicing his fencing moves.

"Hey, Rip!" Alexander called, running over. "Look what I found last night." He opened the notebook. "The worms were warning us about monsters called tunnel fish!"

"Wow," Rip said, reading the page. "So the worms popped up to avoid becoming tunnel-fish bait?" He looked down. "But wait—that means fish monsters are tunneling under us *right now*!"

A dirt pile nearby trembled. Something underneath burrowed straight for the boys.

Alexander stepped back. Rip drew his foil.

POP! A purple fish burst from the ground. It had spiky fins, mean-looking eyes, and a mouthful of teeth. It would have been terrifying, except it was the size of a pickle.

The tunnel fish chomped a worm near Alexander's foot and then dug back underground.

Rip sneered. "Tunnel fish are weenies! We can just smoosh 'em!" He stopped sneering. "Hold on, Salamander . . . what's *that*?"

Another dirt pile rumbled and then — **SPLOTCH!** A silver tunnel fish — the size of a dolphin — shot out of the ground. It swallowed the purple fish in one bite and plowed back underground.

Alexander gulped. "I guess they come in all sizes," he said.

The boys looked at each other and took off running.

CHAPTER 11 CLASH BEFORE CLASS

"How do we fight the tunnel fish?" Rip asked, catching his breath.

"I don't know," said Alexander.

"*There* you are!" said Nikki. She had been pacing outside the gym. "I've been looking for you all morning, Salamander. I —"

"Don't call him *Salamander*!" Rip said through clenched teeth.

Alexander gave a little wave, "Uh. Hi, Nikki."

Nikki turned to face Alexander and Rip.

"I've been watching you," she said. "I know there are monsters in Stermont, and I know you've been fighting them. Last night, I was chased by a fish-creature the size of an alligator!"

Alexander's mouth hung open.

"So what?" said Rip.

Nikki sighed. "So let's work together! I've got some useful, um, skills. And I've been interested in monsters since . . . well, forever."

Alexander nodded. "That sounds —"

"— dumb!" Rip barked. "We don't need your help, hoodie head!"

"Fine!" Nikki said. "But I've also figured out what S.S.M.P. stands for! And now I'm not going to tell you!" She marched into the girls' locker room.

"Forget about her," said Rip. "It's time for our fencing quiz!"

Alexander slapped his forehead. "The quiz is *today*?!"

Rip socked Alexander's arm as they walked into the boys' locker room.

CHAPTER

12 FLOP QUIZ

"Rip, how come you don't like Nikki?" Alexander asked.

"She's weird!" Rip slammed his locker shut. "She's always by herself, she wears that dopey hoodie . . . and now she's following us around!"

Rip looked at the floor. "But that's not the worst part."

Alexander raised an eyebrow. "No?"

"No, Salamander," Rip said. "Last week, that girl crossed the line. The lunch line. There was one dish of Jell-O left . . . and she took it! Right in front of me!"

Alexander laughed. "You're mad because of a little blob of Jell-O?"

Rip frowned. "It was strawberry."

Alexander and Rip walked into class, where students were taking practice swings with their foils. "Rip, you're wrong about Nikki. She's super smart. And brave — she doesn't let you push her around!"

"ALEXANDER BOPP!" shouted a froggy voice. **"DEFEND YOURSELF!"**

A laundry cart shot across the room, straight at Alexander.

Coach Gill stood atop the cart, sword held high.

"Wait, what?!" Alexander cried. He raised his practice foil.

Coach Gill did a backflip off the cart, and — **SMACK!** — swatted Alexander's foil from his hand.

"That was the quiz," she said, "and you *failed*!"

The coach leaned in close, pressing her cold face mask against Alexander's cheek. "You're as weak as Hoarsely," she croaked.

Alexander held his breath. *What was that about?* he thought.

"ALL RIGHT! WHO'S NEXT?" Coach Gill whirled around, bringing her sword down hard.

CLANK!

Her blade clashed against Rip's practice foil. Rip's grip was firm.

"Well done — you've been practicing." Coach Gill lowered her sword. "Rip Bonkowski, you're a model student!"

Rip blinked. Nobody had ever called him that before.

Coach Gill hacked her way down the line, giving everyone an F.

She shook her head. "Pathetic! Only one worthy opponent in the whole class!"

The coach stormed out of the gym.

Alexander dragged Rip over to Nikki, who was picking her foil up off the floor.

"You're right, Nikki," Alexander said. "We should team up. It's the only way to stop these tunnel fish. Right, Rip?"

He gave Rip a nudge.

"I'm, uh," Rip said, gritting his teeth. "I'm sorry you got mad when I called you names and stuff."

Nikki rolled her eyes. "Good enough," she said.

"Great!" said Alexander. "And now, Nikki, can you please tell us what S.S.M.P. stands for?"

"Tell you?" said Nikki. "Better yet, I'll show you! Meet me tonight at the old kickball diamond. 6:30, sharp!"

CHAPTER 13 ON THE WRONG TRACK

CHOMP!

Alexander thought of hungry tunnel fish as he shoveled macaroni into his mouth.

"Mrmmh," he said, scooting his chair back.

"You're finished already?" his dad asked.

"Yeah, Dad." Alexander headed to the door. "I'm meeting my friends in ten minutes."

His dad gave a double thumbs-up. “Good for you, Al! Playing with your new friends . . . Call if you need anything!”

The sun was setting when Alexander arrived at the old kickball diamond.

"Hey, Salamander!"

Rip stood near home plate, talking to a girl Alexander hadn't seen before. She had a long ponytail and was holding a flashlight.

Alexander trotted over. "Hi, I'm Alexan —" He froze. "Wait. *Nikki*? Where's your hoodie?"

Nikki shrugged. "I only wear it during the day."

"Enough chitchat," Rip said. "Tell us what S.S.M.P. stands for!"

"Okay," said Nikki. "Follow me!"

She led the boys through the outfield, stopping near a stretch of rusty railroad track.

"Here we are!" Nikki said. She shone her flashlight on an old train car parked on the tracks — a caboose.

Alexander stared at the initials. "*S.S.M.P.* is a *railroad*?"

"Yep," said Nikki. "It's the old Stermont Superfast Mountain Pacific Railroad. It stopped running years ago."

"What's a run-down railroad got to do with a monster notebook?" asked Rip.

"Beats me," said Alexander. "But there must be a connection! Let's peek inside and —"

BRUMBBUGGRUMMM!

"What's that noise?" Rip asked.

"Look!" Nikki yelled. "The pitcher's mound . . . It's *moving*!"

Just then, a spiky fin burst from the dirt. A scaly beast bulldozed its way toward the kids, chomping everything in its path.

"Run!" shouted Alexander.

CHAPTER 14 HARD TO SWALLOW

The tunnel fish snapped at Alexander's heels. Then Nikki's. Then Rip's.

"A light!" Alexander called out. "Someone's in the caboose!"

They raced over and climbed onto the platform at the back of the caboose.

The tunnel fish stopped at the caboose's metal wheels.

"Ha!" said Rip. "End of the line, sucker!"

The creature opened its toothy mouth.

A moment later, a school of growling tunnel fish began circling the caboose.

"Come on!" said Alexander, catching his breath. "We'll be safer inside."

He knocked on the caboose's back door. It swung open.

"Hello?" Alexander said. No answer.

Alexander stepped inside. A lantern hung from the ceiling, casting light on a strange yellow flag.

"Guys," Alexander said, "you've got to see what's in here."

The three of them inspected the caboose in total silence.

STERMONT
DISGUISES

S.S.M.P.
DON'T GET EATEN!

"Whoa," said Alexander, touching a map on the wall. "What *is* this place?"

"It's a hideout," said a whispery voice.

"Who said that?" Rip asked, looking around.

"It came from that box!" said Nikki, pointing to a large trunk in the corner.

CREEEAK!

The lid of the trunk opened, and Abraham Lincoln slowly rose from inside. Actually, it wasn't Abraham Lincoln. It was a tall, shaky man with a fake beard and top hat.

"Mr. Hoarsely?! What —" Alexander shouted.

"Shhh!" Mr. Hoarsely adjusted his beard. "I'm trying to hide!"

"From the tunnel fish?" asked Rip.

"Tunnel fish?" Mr. Hoarsely peered out the window. "Oh, no! *They're* here?! That means she's tracked me down!" He crouched back into the trunk, letting the lid close.

"*Who's* tracked you down?" asked Alexander.

SLAM! A white boot kicked in the door.

Coach Gill vaulted into the caboose. "AHA! I'VE FOUND YOU!" she shouted, drawing her sword. "REVENGE IS MINE! I — Wait . . ." She looked around. "Where's Hoarsely?"

Alexander shrugged. Rip and Nikki studied the floorboards.

"I know you're hiding him," Coach Gill hissed. "TAKE ME TO HIM — NOW!"

"Mr. Hoarsely?" asked Alexander, leaning against the trunk's lid. "Didn't you say he was on vacation?"

A bone-rattling rumble shook the caboose, swinging the lantern and knocking a pair of skis onto Rip's head. Nikki stumbled, spilling a sack of giant feathers.

Alexander looked out the window in time to see an enormous fish explode through the soil!

Its huge jaws chomped down on all of the surrounding tunnel fish — and the caboose — in one bite.

Alexander gulped.

So did the giant fish.

CHAPTER

15 SLIP OF THE TONGUE

The caboose tumbled about, sending the trunk, papers, binoculars, and a saxophone flying off the shelves before stopping with a **SQUISH!**

"Everyone okay?" Alexander asked.

Rip and Nikki were on the floor. Mr. Hoarsely's trunk was upside down. And Coach Gill was tangled up in a hammock.

Alexander scrambled to a ladder on the wall. "Quick, to the roof!"

The kids climbed to the caboose's rooftop. But instead of seeing the starry night sky, they were greeted by slimy bits of whatever the tunnel fish had eaten for lunch.

"Okay, guys," said Alexander. "Any second now, Coach Gill will cut her way out of that hammock. We're surrounded by small angry tunnel fish, trapped inside the mouth of a giant tunnel fish, and about to be swallowed down into its stomach."

"Then I say, let's go down fighting!" said Nikki.

Rip, for once, smiled at Nikki.

"Good," said Alexander, checking his pockets. "What do we have to defend ourselves with?"

WHO HAS THE BEST WEAPON?

Alexander: A yo-yo!

Rip: A ski pole!

Nikki: A giant feather!

Answer: Nobody. These are all lousy ways to protect yourself from a fish monster attack.

"ENOUGH!" Coach Gill gurgled. She sprung up to the roof, leveling her sword at Alexander. "You've ruined *everything*! After all these years, I was about to destroy the S.S.M.P.!"

"The railroad?" asked Rip.

"No, shrimp brain! S.S.M.P. stands for Super Secret Monster Patrol!"

"So *that's* what it stands for!" said Alexander.

Coach Gill groaned. "And now that I'm stuck in a stupid fish's mouth, I'll *never* get Hoarsely!"

She removed her mask and cut away her armor.

Alexander's jaw dropped. "You're a tunnel fish?" he asked.

"Don't insult me!" said Coach Gill. "Tunnel fish are *beasts*. They obey *me*! I'm a FISH-KABOB!"

The kids took a step back. Coach Gill raised her blade and — **POP!** — she snapped it onto a little opening on her face.

"ALEXANDER BOPP, DEFEND YOURSELF!"

Coach Gill lunged at Alexander, nose-first.

CLACK!

Rip blocked her attack with his ski pole.

"Good save, Rip!" yelled Alexander.

Rip grinned. "Stand back, guys. I've got this."

Coach Gill took a jab at Rip.

"I can't believe I'm fencing with a monster!" Rip said, blocking another thrust.

"We're not fencing . . ." said Coach Gill, ". . . we're sword-fighting!"

"HEE-VAARRGGHH!" Rip let out a battle cry and charged at the fish-kabob. She stepped aside. Rip crashed into his friends, and they all fell off the caboose. They landed on a giant bumpy green tongue, surrounded by growling tunnel fish.

Coach Gill looked down from the roof and laughed. Then she whistled to the small angry tunnel fish. “Dinnertime, my little chums!”

Alexander, Rip, and Nikki stood back-to-back-to-back as the small angry tunnel fish closed in.

Suddenly, Alexander felt his socks getting wet. The giant fish’s mouth was filling with a murky fluid.

“Gross!” said Rip.

“It’s only fish spit,” said Nikki.

The small angry tunnel fish stopped advancing and looked up at Coach Gill. “Keep going!” she commanded. “Eat them! EAT!”

SLUURGHHH!

The ground buckled. The giant tunnel fish mashed its tongue against the roof of its mouth, squeezing the children and knocking Coach Gill off the caboose.

The tunnel fish crowded around Coach Gill, whimpering.

Alexander got to his knees. "Look! They're afraid!"

"Afraid of what?" asked Nikki.

A wave of slobber flooded the giant fish mouth.

"Of getting swallowed down into the giant fish's belly!" yelled Alexander.

CHAPTER 16 BLAAARF!

"What do we do?" Rip gasped.

Alexander looked at the yo-yo in his hand: *It's awesome to floss 'em.*

He gave the yo-yo a hard spin outward, and — **CLONK!** — yanked down, wedging it between two giant teeth.

"Grab on!" Alexander cried. He held fast to the yo-yo as Rip and Nikki hugged his legs.

The fish gulped down its mouthful, washing Coach Gill and the small angry tunnel fish down its throat.

The kids and caboose stayed put.

"Holy mackerel," said Alexander. "It worked!"

"We're lucky your dad's a dentist!" said Nikki.

Rip wiped slime off his face. "Okay," he said, "we didn't get swallowed, but we're still stuck in a fish mouth!"

"Oh yeah?" said Nikki. "Watch this!" She wiggled the giant feather on the fish's tongue.

The tongue quivered for a second. Then —

The giant fish spewed the kids and caboose out onto dry land. Then it tunneled back into the ground.

"If the notebook's right, that giant tunnel fish should sleep for 99 years now," said Alexander. "I'm pretty sure eating Coach Gill and all of the other tunnel fish counts as a big meal."

The kids looked around. They were in the middle of a forest.

"Hey," said Rip. "We're in Gobbler's Woods. Look, Salamander, that's your house!"

CREAK!

Mr. Hoarsely climbed down from the caboose.

"First, it was the balloon goons," he moaned. "Then the worms, the tunnel fish, and a phone threat from a fish-kabob. I can't take it anymore! I quit!"

"Quit what?" Nikki asked.

"The Super Secret Monster Patrol," said Mr. Hoarsely. "Congratulations. You kids are in charge now. You've already got the notebook, and here's your headquarters." He nodded toward the drool-covered caboose. "Oh, you'll need this," he added. He handed Alexander a ripped sheet of notebook paper.

"But wait —" said Alexander.

"What about —" asked Rip.

"Where were —" began Nikki.

"Tut!" said Mr. Hoarsely. "I'm dizzy, cold, and up past my bedtime. Good luck battling the next monster, leap-year boy!" He looked into Alexander's eyes, and then staggered away.

Alexander held up the paper. "It's the missing page from the notebook!"

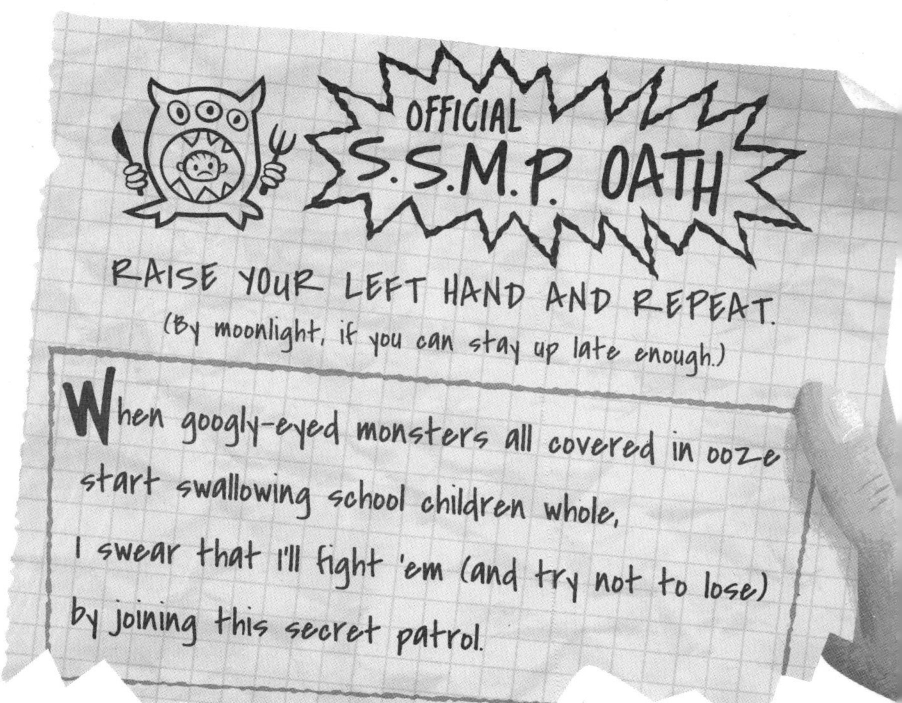

"An oath?" asked Nikki. "Should we all swear to it?"

"Yes," said Alexander. He held up his left hand. "Stermont is counting on us."

The three slimy friends recited the oath.

Then Alexander completed his first official task as leader of the Super Secret Monster Patrol: He added another monster to the notebook.

FISH-KABOB

A scaly monster with
a sword for a nose.

SILENCE! Fish-kabobs are bossy, especially to tunnel fish.

HABITAT Hospital laundry rooms?

DIET Tuna salad, from the smell of things.

BEHAVIOR Fish-kabobs are master ~~sword-fighters~~ fencers. They can unscrew their sword-noses to disguise themselves as regular people.

WARNING! Don't fight a fish-kabob unless you've had more than one fencing lesson!

TROY CUMMINGS

has no tail, no wings, no fangs, no claws, and only one head. As a kid, he believed that monsters might really exist. Today, he's sure of it.

BEHAVIOR This creature is a terrible dancer, although he doesn't seem to be aware of this fact.

HABITAT Troy Cummings spends most of his time in a creepy old building that makes weird sounds.

DIET Pastrami sandwich with Swiss cheese and peppers.

EVIDENCE Few people believe that Troy Cummings is real. The only proof we have is that he supposedly wrote and illustrated The Eensy-Weensy Spider Freaks Out! and Giddy-up, Daddy!

WARNING! Keep your eyes peeled for more danger in The Notebook of Doom #3:

ATTACK OF THE SHADOW SMASHERS